SEARCHING FOR SIGNIFICANCE

Searching for Significance: A Devotional Journey Through Ecclesiastes
Copyright © 2020 Matthew Geib.

ISBN-13: 978-1733174794

Published by Lazarus Tribe Media, LLC
Rome, Georgia, USA
www.lazarustribe.media

Edited by Rachel Newman

Unless otherwise indicated, Scripture quotations are taken from the New American Standard Bible® (NASB), Copyright © 1960, 1962, 1963, 1968, 1971, 1972, 1973, 1975, 1977, 1995 by The Lockman Foundation. Used by permission. www.Lockman.org

Scripture quotations marked (HCSB) are taken from the Holman Christian Standard Bible®, Used by Permission HCSB ©1999,2000,2002,2003,2009 Holman Bible Publishers. Holman Christian Standard Bible®, Holman CSB®, and HCSB® are federally registered trademarks of Holman Bible Publishers.

Scripture quotations marked (AMPC) are taken from the Amplified® Bible (AMPC), Copyright © 1954, 1958, 1962, 1964, 1965, 1987 by The Lockman Foundation. Used by permission. www.Lockman.org

Scripture quotations marked (NLT) are taken from THE HOLY BIBLE, NEW LIVING TRANSLATION, Copyright© 1996, 2004, 2007 by Tyndale House Foundation. Used by permission of Tyndale House Publishers, Inc., Carol Stream, Illinois 60188. All rights reserved. Used by permission.

Scripture quotations marked (KJV) are taken from the KING JAMES VERSION, public domain.

Scripture quotations marked (Darby) are taken from the DARBY BIBLE, published in 1867, 1872, 1884, 1890; public domain.

SEARCHING
FOR
SIGNIFICANCE
A Devotional Journey
Through Ecclesiastes

By Matthew P. Geib

Lazarus Tribe Media
Rome, Georgia

TABLE OF CONTENTS

About The Author

Matthew P. Geib is a Minister and Teacher of the Gospel of Jesus Christ. He has taught as a compassionate and exegetical Bible Teacher in several churches over the past 40 years. Matt is also a father, grandfather, and loving husband residing 40 miles southeast of Seattle, Washington.

Currently, he is the founder of "The Kingdom Corner," a podcast that airs several times each month. Matthew is available to teach or speak at conferences throughout the year.

CONTACT:

Email: matthewpgeib@gmail.com

www.significanceacademy.com

www.kingdom-corner.com

Preface

The beginning of what I call my writer's journey for this devotional book was birthed within me over 60 years ago in the spring of 1958 when I was adopted by my mother, a "PK" (Preacher's Kid). I was brought up in the Midwest, in a very conservative Christian home. We went to the local Presbyterian church every Sunday, where I first learned of the Love of Jesus and committed my life to Him publicly when I was nine years of age at a Billy Graham movie. I have been a Bible Teacher for 48 years in several churches and even served as a Pastor for ten years in one fellowship. Being a student of God's Word, around 20 years ago, I began an intensive study of the Book of Ecclesiastes and taught a Wednesday evening class about Solomon, Proverbs, and Ecclesiastes for three years. This book, *Searching For Significance: A Devotional Journey Through Ecclesiastes*, came to fruition this past summer. It is not only based on my years of study on the topic, but fresh, timely, and inspirational insights the Father has given me over the past 18 months through my association with Pastor, Teacher, and author Tyler Frick, and Rachel Newman, founder of Lazarus Tribe Media.

Meeting these two individuals, plus many other like-minded saints from The King's Company (a fellowship created by Pastor Tyler in 2018), has breathed fresh new life into my Christian experience and given me the boldness and courage to share the message I carry within me for the 21st Century Church.

When I began to write this book, it was just to be a meditative devotional experience for me as I was reading through Ecclesiastes in my daily devotions. It seemed God began to give me fresh insight and revelation that I began to commit to my daily journal. In those contemplative times, I could start to see the need for others to glean from the encouragement God was giving me. For many, a devotional book on Ecclesiastes may seem absurd because so many Bible scholars and students know how melancholy and cynical Solomon is throughout his treatise on the "Vanity of Life under the sun," as he called his daily experiences toward the end of his life. However, this is the very heart of the message that I see in Ecclesiastes that makes it such a significant and timely story for us! Our lives today, even though 2900 years removed from the time of Ecclesiastes, are not any different.

We are all on a search, as Solomon was, to find the meaning and purpose of life. At times, we also sit back in smug and seemingly apathetic denial, saying to our friends, "All is well with my soul," when in fact, we are hurting and crying inside. Solomon's Ecclesiastes is a desperate, authentic, and unashamed cry to find meaning and purpose in life on this earth.

I so appreciate the honesty I have found within this book. Yes, Solomon is very vocal in saying over 30 times that life and what he is experiencing is "Meaninglessness," without purpose; for me, that is where our own personal "Search for Significance" must begin. I would ask you, the reader, to be honest. If you find your life currently without dreams to live for, or you have lost your way like a ship without a rudder drifting along, then my prayer is that this simple book about Solomon's pursuit of the meaning of life will compel you to see all that God has for you. Something significant, at times, is not always self-evident or easily recognized by us in all the confusion and chaos that we experience in life. Now is your time to find what is significant for you and about you as a unique individual God has created for a purpose. He is waiting to take your hand and walk with you on this journey.

Since I first began in July 2019 to write the meditations of what would become this book, the times and seasons we find ourselves living in have definitely changed. We are currently in a season where Solomon would say, "We must Consider the Day of Adversity" that COVID-19 has brought into our lives.

I believe we are now in a "parenthesis" in our lives where God wants us to seriously sit down and contemplate what He would have us do both individually and as a Nation. Hopefully, this crisis can be similar to "the slap in the face" that the message of Ecclesiastes can be at times, where God is wanting to wake us all up and say:

"Here I Am.

I am God!

I am in control.

I am here for you if you just turn to Me!"

other and our family on Mom's and Dad's side. I hope you will find his message as inspirational as I do.

Love,
Helene

July 6, 2022

Dear Judy,
   I want you to have a copy of this booklet. Upon my mom's death 16 years ago I began a correspondence with her cousin Vera. Vera lived in Ohio, as she aged into her middle eighties she moved to the state of Washington and lived with her son. Vera died last month at home. God blessed me by reconnecting with Matthew, Vera's son. Matthew graciously sent me a copy of his booklet. We have begun to correspond and are learning about each

1

A Searcher Searches

Ecclesiastes 1:1

The words of the Preacher. The son of King David, King in Jerusalem.

Today is the beginning of a devotional journey through my favorite Old Testament book of the Bible, Ecclesiastes. Appropriately, we start with the very first verse of the entire book, which encapsulates for us in five simple words the meaning of the 12 chapters that are Ecclesiastes. We identify the author right away by the second and third phrases of this verse. "The son of King David, the King in Jerusalem." We can see that it was David's son, Solomon, who succeeded him as King of Israel.

Though it is true David had other sons, only Solomon was ever recognized as the rightful heir to his throne.

"The words of the Preacher" upon closer examination can unlock for us the purpose and intention that Solomon may have aspired to when penning this book 2900 years ago. In the original language of Hebrew that this book was written in, the word for "Preacher" is "Qoheleth" pronounced, kō ·heh' ·leth. A better rendering or meaning in our English language would be "Searcher," or one that searches for, assembles, or correlates and collects data for observations and conclusive ideas about a topic. Ecclesiastes' theme then is all about Solomon's often desperate and frustrating search for the significance of life.

It has never ceased to amaze me over the years the paradox portrayed throughout this mysterious and tantalizing book. On the one hand, we can see from Scripture that at Solomon's inauguration as king, God granted him more Wisdom than any man ever had or will have (outside of Jesus Christ) again in this life. However, here he was in his musings in Ecclesiastes seemingly lost, not having a clue about life and its purpose.

This book represents a very dark time in the king's life, written most likely in the last 10-15 years of his life (Solomon lived to be 60 years old) and reign as king. Ecclesiastes represents for us the loss of light and revelation that God can bestow on a man or woman. Solomon, the wisest and richest man on the planet, fully blessed by God, the counselor other kings and nations looked to for wisdom and guidance, somewhere over the years had drifted away from his close, personal relationship with God. As we study his life, we can see that various issues like foreign women (he married foreign women he was told by God NOT to marry), riches, and arrogance caused him to lose his focus on God and fall away and lose the enlightenment he once had. Solomon's plight also reminds me of John The Baptist, who came as a zealous prophet crying out of the wilderness, heralding the ministry of Jesus. Yet, sadly, at the end of his life, we find John in prison questioning who Jesus was, whether or not He was the Promised Messiah, for he had lost the light he once possessed.

SIGNIFICANCE:

The lesson for us today is that no matter how much God has touched our lives, healed our hearts and bodies, restored us, given us wonderful experiences of His Love, I believe we can easily allow hurts and distractions we face to cause us to grow distant from Him. Also, sometimes unconfronted issues we continue to carry get in the way as well, or just because of the everyday cares of our lives. We must continue to follow the Father daily, always seeking His heart in humility and openness. The revelation God has given us today is not enough to sustain us for tomorrow. We must, like the Israelites in the wilderness, have FRESH manna from Him at the dawning of each new day.

2

The Meaninglessness of Life

Ecclesiastes 1:2

Vanity of Vanities, saith the Preacher, all is vanity

So right away in the very first part of Ecclesiastes, we find Solomon's conclusion about the meaning of life, which he then outlines for us in the next 12 chapters of his search.

Solomon states, "All Is Vanity." Again, the Hebrew word for "vanity" here provides for us a much richer and provocative meaning. The root word, "hebel," literally means "breath" or "vapor," and alludes to the idea of something being empty and worthless. This definition is why some translations say "meaninglessness." Redundantly, throughout the next 12 chapters, the phrase "Vanity of Vanities," or "meaninglessness of meaninglessness," is repeated 37 times! To Solomon, all things in life had become meaningless, worthless, of no lasting value.

Solomon was the "Jeff Bezos" of his day, the wealthiest man in the world. He states in Ecclesiastes 2:10 that all that his eyes saw and his heart and mind desired he obtained! Yet STILL to him, it was all empty and without meaning. He had come to the place where he found no real purpose for which to live or exist anymore.

For reasons like this that Solomon states so negatively, many Bible scholars believe Ecclesiastes should not have been included in the 66 books of the Bible. Many have come to believe that God did not inspire the writing of Ecclesiastes since the content seems so opposite of God's redemptive message. However, I conclude the very opposite to be true. God very much desired its inclusion in the Canon of Scripture if, for no other reason, than to show how all humans are prone, at times, to look at life in such hopeless ways without God in the picture.

Many in the Christian community are quick to condemn Solomon as he was blessed with wealth and wisdom beyond any other human living. They wonder how could such a person who had everything money could buy, as well as being the most gifted genius alive, see life as pointless.

And yet, seeing life as day-to-day drudgery with no real purpose or meaning is a state most every person (if not all people) will experience at least some time in their lives. You lose employment, seemingly out of the blue your spouse leaves you, a friend or loved one dies suddenly. Or possibly you wake up one day and realize how long the days have been, yet bitterly how swift the years have flown by, and you have no real meaning to show for them at 60 years old.

Where, oh where, did all those years go!? Has your life been a total LOSS!? Without any real Purpose or Meaning!?

Even many folks like Solomon, who have reached the pinnacle of unimaginable wealth and fame, come to the conclusion that money and notoriety are empty and devoid of any lasting meaning. In the end, these things pass away or, as Solomon observed, someone dies, and their wealth passes on to another.

I believe it is beneficial for all of us to experience those "Meaninglessness of Meaninglessness" thoughts and feelings about life. They will (if we allow them to) force us to honestly search for the meaning and purpose our lives were meant to embrace.

In Matthew 7:7 (KJV) Jesus said this:

Ask and it shall be given you; seek and ye shall find; knock and it shall be opened to you.

In the original Greek language of the New Testament, the text reads:

Keep on Seeking, Keep on ASKING, Keep on Knocking.

SIGNIFICANCE:

Our search for the significance of Life and its Meaning is always ONGOING. To find meaning and purpose takes TIME and EFFORT.

However, we find the most crucial ingredient in our search is to ASK of The Father and not to neglect Him in our searching and asking of questions about life.

Matthew 7:11 KJV

...how much more shall your Father which is in heaven give good things to them that ask him?

Unlike Solomon, we must not turn from our heavenly Father, allowing the issues of life to keep us away from Him. If we trust Him, we will find again and again what we were created for.

So, NEVER GIVE UP!

Do not succumb to despair. Allow your feelings of utter hopelessness (Meaninglessness of Meaninglessness) to drive you to persistently ASK, SEEK, and KNOCK until the Father opens the door of meaning and purpose for you!

3

Of Times and Seasons

Ecclesiastes 3:1-8 (KJV)

For everything there is a season, and a time for every matter under heaven: a time to be born, and a time to die; a time to plant, and a time to pluck up what is planted; a time to kill, and a time to heal; a time to break down, and a time to build up; a time to weep, and a time to laugh; a time to mourn, and a time to dance; a time to cast away stones, and a time to gather stones together; a time to embrace, and a time to refrain from embracing; a time to seek, and a time to lose; a time to keep, and a time to cast away; a time to tear, and a time to sew; a time to keep silent, and a time to speak; a time to love, and a time to hate; a time for war, and a time for peace.

Here we have possibly some of the most well-known verses in the Bible today, made famous in 1965 by the rock-and-roll group, The Byrds. This portion of Scripture was crafted into a song by folk singer Pete Seeger in the late 1950s, and in 1965 The Byrds recorded it, and it went on to become a #1 Hit on the music charts. Seeger wrote the song titled "Turn, Turn, Turn," verbatim from this passage, only adding his own last six words, "I swear it's not too late."

A time to love, and a time to hate; a time of war, and a time of peace. What Seeger and The Byrds intended the song to be was a plea for world peace, hence Seeger's admonition that it was "not too late."

Much could be said about desiring a "season" of world peace. My feeling is that this world will not attain a season of lasting and eternal peace until Jesus Christ returns the second time and establishes a New Heaven and Earth (Revelation 21:1-7). But I want to explore for a moment the importance, as Seeger states, of NOT being TOO LATE.

As the line of this song reminds us, we can miss out on a "season" or a "time" in life and be too late to experience what was intended, or worse yet make a mess of a situation through acting in an ill-timed manner, out of season, as it were.

Essentially, the words "Season" and "Time" in this passage mean just that, the idea of a SPECIFIC, or an APPOINTED time. It is interesting to me that in the Heavenly Realm, "Time," as we know it, does not exist, and yet God has placed us in a world where definite "blocks of time" really matter.

Perhaps God desired to show us a paradox in creating time in this life. In our finite lives on earth, we all measure the passing of our lives by increments of time measured in minutes, hours, days, months, and years. As we get older, the passage of time seems to speed up with each fleeting year, 'til we may wonder where all our life's years went! Could the very idea of passing periods of "time" and "seasons" as Solomon conveys here in these eight verses be a clue for us to see the existence of the eternal realm?

There are many defining moments throughout our finite lives like birth, celebrations, war, love, planting and harvesting crops, etc., that all humanity experiences. We see that various events and experiences mark the importance of our lives on earth, and yet someday, for us all, these events of time will end, and our bodies will wither and pass away. I believe God has impregnated within every person the realization deep down that there is an eternity. Solomon himself goes onto say in verse 11 that "He has placed ETERNITY in man's heart." To me, this very paradox of TIME in which we exist here in this earthly realm, yet with no existence of time in the Heavenly realm, speaks to us that there is something more, something better for which God created us. And if we will allow our hearts to grasp this, we will see that we were created to be eternal beings with a spirit to have an eternal relationship of love and intimacy with the heavenly Father, Who created all things, even TIME.

Therefore, it behooves each of us in this life to "be on time." 1 Chronicles 12:32 is an intriguing passage that says the sons (tribe) of Issachar were men who understood the times, with knowledge of what Israel should do. This life, which consists of TIME and the importance of various passing events, is meant to ultimately point each man and woman to the existence of ETERNITY, which never ends, and the offer from the heavenly Father of a Life filled with Love and intimacy with Him, which will never end. To understand the purpose of time is to know that we must pursue a relationship with Him as we pass throughout all the seasons and experiences of life!

Notice these verses:

Luke 2:11

today in the city of David there has been born for you a Savior, who is Christ the Lord.

There was a day, an appointed TIME Jesus was born, yet many of His countrymen missed it.

Luke 4:18-19, 21

"THE SPIRIT OF THE LORD IS UPON ME, BECAUSE HE ANOINTED ME TO PREACH THE GOSPEL TO THE POOR. HE HAS SENT ME TO PROCLAIM RELEASE TO THE CAPTIVES, AND RECOVERY OF SIGHT TO THE BLIND, TO SET FREE THOSE WHO ARE OPPRESSED,

To proclaim the acceptable Year of our Lord

And He began to say to them, "Today this Scripture has been fulfilled in your hearing."

There was a day Jesus was commissioned to begin His ministry, and again many refused Him and missed out on His season of service.

Hebrews 3:7,15, 4:7

TODAY if you will hear his voice...

Hebrews 3:13

Encourage one another day after day while it is still called TODAY

Scripture places great importance on always HEAR-ING the Father and encouraging the Brethren TODAY... because we may not have tomorrow!

2 Corinthians 6:2

NOW is the DAY of salvation...

SIGNIFICANCE:

NOW is the day to answer God's call. Not tomorrow or next week. You may not have such conviction tomorrow or next week; you may have even left this world.

These scriptures are just a few that speak of the importance of Time or Seasons. "To everything there is a time or season," Solomon penned. My question is, are we aware of the Times and Seasons in which God has placed us? Are we on-time with the plan of God for our lives?

I Chronicles 12:32

Of the sons of Issachar, men who understood the times, with knowledge of what Israel should do,

I Thessalonians 5:1-8

Now as to the times and the epochs, brethren, you have no need of anything to be written to you. For you yourselves know full well that the day of the Lord will come just like a thief in the night. While they are saying, "Peace and safety!" then destruction will come upon them suddenly like labor pains upon a woman with child, and they will not escape. But you, brethren, are not in darkness, that the day would overtake you like a thief; for you are all sons of light and sons of day. We are not of night nor of darkness; so then let us not sleep as others do, but let us be alert and sober. For those who sleep do their sleeping at night, and those who get drunk get drunk at night. But since we are of the day, let us be sober, having put on the breastplate of faith and love, and as a helmet, the hope of salvation.

4

Eternity, The Undiscovered Country

Ecclesiastes 3:11

He has made everything appropriate in its time. He has also set eternity in their heart, yet so that man will not find out the work which God has done from the beginning to the end.

This past week as a family, we spent several evenings watching special TV telecasts of our nation landing on the Moon. Saturday, June 20th was the 50th anniversary when Neil Armstrong first set foot on the Moon, exclaiming, "One small step for Man, One giant leap for Mankind." In this simple verse that Solomon expressed, I believe, spiritually speaking, we can see so much from our nation's space exploration that parallels our own spiritual journey.

In this example from Ecclesiastes, "ETERNITY" represents the Moon. Since inception into the Kingdom of God as His children, based on our acceptance of Jesus Christ as our Savior, we have commenced a journey to set foot on ETERNITY. We know when we pass away someday, we will literally be in ETERNITY (Heaven). I would say that God setting or placing ETERNITY "in our hearts" signifies a journey that can begin for us all when we enter His Kingdom IF we choose to venture to the "MOON," to the eternal realm each day.

Every person from the most wicked (Hitler, Stalin) to the Most Saintly (Billy Graham, Mother Teresa) has had God place or SET (like a hook) eternity in his or her heart the moment He created them.

Like animals migrating or hibernating, each of us was created with an innate need or desire for God. We have a knowing that there is a Creator Who desires a relationship with us. However, what we do with that desire is a personal choice that God gave us. We can deny that longing all of our lives, or choose to take that journey to experience the ETERNITY He set in our hearts.

For many of us travelers on this eternal spiritual journey, we have been taught that it begins and ends with salvation in Jesus Christ. We've believed that we could not truly comprehend the depths and beauty of Eternity until we pass away from this life and join the heavenly host around God's throne. However, I have come to disagree with that view and I remain convinced there is so much more we can taste and experience of the ETERNAL realm even while still on this planet. There is such a more profound connection we can have with ETERNITY than we may have ever realized was possible!

Here is how Paul expressed this:

Ephesians 3:16-20 (AMPC)

May He grant you out of the riches of His glory, to be strengthened and spiritually energized with power through His Spirit in your inner self, [indwelling your innermost being and personality], so that Christ may dwell in your hearts through your faith. And may you, having been [deeply] rooted and [securely] grounded in love, be fully capable of comprehending with all the saints (God's people) the width and length and height and depth of His love [fully experiencing that amazing, endless love]; and [that you may come] to know [practically, through personal experience] the love of Christ which far surpasses [mere] knowledge [without experience], that you may be filled up [throughout your being] to all the fullness of God [so that you may have the richest experience of God's presence in your lives, completely filled and flooded with God Himself]. Now to Him who is able to [carry out His purpose and] do superabundantly more than all that we dare ask or think [infinitely beyond our greatest prayers, hopes, or dreams], according to His power that is at work within us,

Simply stated, we can KNOW and experience the depths of God's LOVE in this life. This Love flows from the realms of Eternity.

Today's devotional is titled, "ETERNITY...The Undiscovered Country," just like the old StarTrek movie where peace with an arch-enemy was being sought out and called the Undiscovered Country. Experiencing Eternity here in this life for us is an undiscovered country, just waiting for us to pursue it, discover it, and taste it!

Paul quotes the Old Testament Prophet Isaiah to reveal this truth:

1 Corinthians 2:9-10

but just as it is written, "Things which eye has not seen and ear has not heard, And which have not entered the heart of man, All that God has prepared for those who love Him." For to us God revealed them through the Spirit; for the Spirit searches all things, even the depths of God.

Did you catch the phrase in verse 10? God revealed these unheard of and unseen truths to us in our spirits here and now. They are not something only reserved for Heaven!

SIGNIFICANCE:

The depths of the riches of God's Truth and Love await our discovery. Yes, they may be undiscovered today, but if we pursue them, God will surely reveal them to us!

Proverbs 25:2

It is the glory of God to conceal a matter, But the glory of kings is to search out a matter.

Will we choose today to be those "Kings" searching out the Riches of Eternity?

5

What Do You Desire?

Ecclesiastes 2:10

All that my eyes desired I did not refuse them, I did not withhold my heart from any pleasure...

Imagine for a moment that you are in Solomon's shoes. You can have anything your heart desires or eyes behold. What if you won the Powerball Sweepstakes, just what would you do? Would you be like Solomon, buying any item or experience that you fancied? Some say money alone does not change an individual; it just brings out more of who they already are.

I could sit here and tell you all the dos and don'ts of accumulating money and possessions based on what I learned years and years within the church. Things like, "money is the root of all evil," and "money will keep you out of heaven," etc. And some of that may be true, yet not always... However, I do think in many ways we might be no different than Solomon, embarking on a spending spree to amass new houses, cars, and travel the world. Money, in many ways, is a test that judges our hearts and motives. Jesus said in Matthew 6:21, "For where your treasure is, there will your heart be also."

As Jesus said, our hearts determine our desires. If we are consumed with earthly possessions, fame, and money, that is what we will pursue. Ironically, Solomon's utmost desire when he became king 20 years earlier was Wisdom from God. He didn't ask for riches; he wanted wisdom for how to reign and rule the kingdom God gave him. In asking for wisdom, God threw in as a bonus Solomon's wealth (1 Kings 3:5-15). Now all these years later, riches and pleasure have consumed him, and he had sadly come to the conclusion it was all in vain and "meaninglessness." In thinking further on this passage, 1 John 2:15-17 comes to my mind also; it is, for me, the New Testament counterpart to what Solomon said and experienced.

1 John 2:15-17

Do not love the world nor the things in this world. If anyone loves the world, the love of the father is not in him. For all that is in the world, the lust of the flesh and the lust of the eyes and the boastful pride of life, is not from the Father, but is from the world. The world is passing away, and also its lusts; but the one who does the will of God lives forever.

Solomon had succumbed to the base desires of his FLESH. As John said, the lust of his flesh and his eyes, as well as a desire for prideful worldly recognition, began to replace his desire for God. He had begun to use the riches God had gifted to him to appease his flesh-ly desires, to obtain anything that he felt might please him and make him look good in man's eyes.

These desires are, sadly, a trap most of the world is caught up in, even we as Christians can be side-tracked by "the love of the world." We must realize as Solomon's father, David, said: real, lasting joy and fulfillment could only come by being in the Father's presence.

Psalm 16:11

You will make known to me the path of life, In Your presence is fullness of joy; In Your right hand there are pleasures forevermore.

Is having wealth and possessions wrong? I would say no, however, your HEART will determine what you will do with that wealth. We can use our money to do good things like feeding the poor or advance the Gos-pel message. We need saints who can handle money and be good stewards of the funds God bestows upon them. In this book of Ecclesiastes, Solomon shows, through his quest for answers about the most meaning-ful things in life, that he had lost focus on the Source of meaning: The Father. He allowed wealth, possessions, and the experiences his status brought him to become the dominant theme in how he lived each day, over his relationship with the Father. I would say it takes dis-cipline to keep your focus on "things that are above" continually, the ETERNAL realm, a relationship with our heavenly Father, and not all the things (seemingly good or bad) going on about you every day (See Colos-sians 3:2). Paul gives us a great example of this needed focus and discipline to obtain the heavenly realm, and the Glory that awaits us there, in 1 Corinthians 9:24-27. He references the Olympic Games in Greece and an athlete participating in a race. He speaks of this athlete maintaining physical discipline over his body to obtain a "perishable wreath." Of how much more value is that crown of Glory we will one day receive in Eternity? Or, for that matter, how much more rewarding to maintain daily communion with our Father above!

SIGNIFICANCE:

We must determine and commit to allowing God to consume us with a desire for His Word, His Presence, and to do His will more than we desire wealth and possessions and earthly experiences.

Psalm 19:7-10

The law of the Lord is perfect, restoring the soul; The testimony of the Lord is sure, making wise the simple. The precepts of the Lord are right, rejoicing the heart; The commandment of the Lord is pure, enlightening the eyes. The fear of the Lord is clean, enduring forever; The judgments of the Lord are true; they are righteous altogether. They are more desirable than gold, yes, than much fine gold; Sweeter also than honey and the drippings of the honeycomb.

Psalm 84:10

For a day in Your courts is better than a thousand outside. I would rather stand at the threshold of the house of my God Than dwell in the tents of wickedness.

John 4:34

Jesus saith unto them, "My meat is to do the will of him that sent me, and to finish his work."

Philippians 3:10-14

that I may know Him and the power of His

resurrection and the fellowship of His suffer-ings, being conformed to His death; 11 in or-der that I may attain to the resurrection from the dead. Not that I have already obtained it or have already become perfect, but I press on so that I may lay hold of that for which I was laid hold of by Christ Jesus. Brethren, I do not regard myself as having laid hold of it yet; but one thing I do: forgetting what lies behind and reaching forward to what lies ahead, I press on toward the goal for the prize of the upward call of God in Christ Jesus.

6

And They Have No Comforter

Ecclesiastes 4:1 (NIV)

*Again I looked and saw all the oppression
that was taking place under the sun:
I saw the tears of the oppressed --
and they have no comforter; power
was on the side of the oppressors
-- and they have no comforter.*

I remember almost 20 years ago when I landed in India for the first time on a missionary trip. I stepped off the bus next to our hotel in the middle of a very humid evening, and my system was immediately shocked by both the oppression I felt and saw, even though it was a pitch-black night. There was a multitude of bodies lying within a few feet of me sleeping on the streets; later, I found they had nowhere else to go. Garbage and refuse were piled high all around me; again, I was told there was nowhere else for it to go. India indeed was a nation of people under oppression; even the very air carried a scent of abusive hopelessness. Perhaps this is similar to what Solomon was experiencing when he penned this verse.

Notice the phrase, "Under The Sun" (used over 20 times in Ecclesiastes). These three words highlight Solomon's focus throughout the book. Of course, this is Solomon referring to his view of the world. He has a "world view," an "under the sun view," without consideration of God, and so this was a view of hopelessness for the oppressed, as he notes twice no comfort or comforter is available to bring hope and change for the better. It seems since the fallen world has existed, there has been oppression by others or by life's circumstances.

The word used in this text for oppressed and oppression in the Hebrew language connotes all the following: extortion, violence enacted on another to defraud them of what is rightfully theirs, ill-gotten gain, to crush or press, and also "to drink up."

Sadly our world is full of many "oppressors:" people who want to control others and force them to submit. They extort possessions as well as everything relating to personhood, like a blood-sucking leech drinking up all the life in another.

Also, in contrast to oppression in this passage, the Searcher is lamenting that he sees no "Comforter." He felt all the power was held by the oppressors so much so that he asserts twice, "There is NO Comforter."

The word for "Comforter" here means to be moved with pity to bring consolation, comfort, and compassion to another in need. For all the oppression Solomon sees, he has no hope that there is anyone to arrive and bring the needed succor into this situation. Immediately as I ponder this scene, I am asking why in the world would Solomon, both the richest and wisest man in the world, NOT step forward with a solution? Surely he could have been a comforter with both monies and wisdom to alleviate this issue, or at least improve it. It is interesting to note here, about ten years ago, Bill Gates and Warren Buffett (two of the five wealthiest men in all the world) joined forces and proclaimed that with their wealth, they wanted to eliminate poverty in their lifetime. Solomon's very name meant "PEACE," he had the ability and resources to provide a solution and bring comfort, yet dolefully, he sat on the sidelines.

It is so evident in this passage how far Solomon has fallen from his throne of light. He himself was the best solution available, yet he did nothing! He was so deceived that in the next verse, he says the dead are better off than the living.

So having related all of this, where does it leave you and me? The first thought that comes to mind is Jesus' words:

Matthew 5:14-16

"You are the light of the world. A city set on a hill cannot be hidden; nor does anyone light a lamp and put it under a basket, but on the lampstand, and it gives light to all who are in the house. Let your light shine before men in such a way that they may see your good works, and glorify your Father who is in heaven.

As Christians who love God, we must not be complacent as we see all those who are victims of oppression; instead, we must "let our lights shine," which means providing consolation, comfort, and even liberation to the oppressed. Light offers not only warmth and comfort but enlightenment in how to remedy a situation where there is seemingly no hope.

Romans 15:13

Now may the God of hope fill you with all joy and peace in believing, so that you will abound in hope by the power of the Holy Spirit.

Finally, as God's sons and daughters, we are never without hope as we are never without a Comforter. One of Jesus' most precious promises to His disciples as well as us today is: I will pray the Father, and He shall give you another COMFORTER, that he may abide with you forever (John 14:16). The COMFORTER promised to us is the Holy Spirit (John 14:26). Not only is the Holy Spirit, THE COMFORTER, leading, guiding, and comforting us through any adversity we may encounter, He gives us that same ability to be a COMFORT to others and deliver them from oppression. In the passage here in Ecclesiastes, the root meaning for "comforter" (nacham) is "to breathe." The word in Greek used for spirit, like Holy Spirit, is "pneuma;" again, it also means BREATH or to BREATHE. As Christians, we possess the BREATH of God's life-giving Spirit that brings comfort, as well as freedom from bondage that may attempt to assail us. Again, we also have the ability to breathe LIFE into another person or situation, giving LIFE where once there was hopeless oppression.

2 Corinthians 1:3-4 (NASB)

Blessed be the God and Father of our Lord Jesus Christ, the Father of mercies and God of all comfort, who comforts us in all our affliction so that we will be able to comfort those who are in any affliction with the comfort with which we ourselves are comforted by God.

SIGNIFICANCE:

As Men and Women of God, we carry a SOLUTION for people in need of comfort and help who may cross our paths daily. In Luke 17:21 (KJV), Jesus said, "The Kingdom of God Is Within YOU!"

Jesus sent the disciples out two-by-two to do the work of the Kingdom: healing the sick, delivering people from demons, raising the dead, and blessing households by showing love and meeting basic needs.

THIS is the work of the KINGDOM!

You man/woman of God carry that same KING-DOM, life-transforming power within you to bring life and hope to others. Do not be as Solomon and look at others' problems hopelessly.

Be the solution for someone today!

7

Two Are Better Than One

Ecclesiastes 4:9-12 (KJV)

Two are better than one; because they have a good reward for their labour. For if they fall, the one will lift up his fellow: but woe to him that is alone when he falleth; for he hath not another to help him up. Again, if two lie together, then they have heat: but how can one be warm alone? And if one prevail against him, two shall withstand him; and a threefold cord is not quickly broken.

An example of such loneliness from the 1960s is billionaire Howard Hughes, who passed away in 1972. At the end of his life, he looked like a disheveled bum. There ended up being so many relatives and others laying claim to his wealth it took over 15 years to settle his estate. What a sad ending of solitude and loneliness to a promising life that could have benefitted so many! It really is true as the rock-and-roll group Three Dog Night sang in the 1970s, "One is the loneliest number that you ever do…"

This "man-all-alone" theme then segues into an answer to this loneliness: having a true friend to lean on along the way throughout the challenges we face in an uncertain life. "Two are better than one." Having, as my Dad would have said, "A running buddy." Solomon notes several advantages that the person walking alone can never have.

- If you fall, your friend can be there to pick you up.

- Two lying together keep warm.

This is a metaphor for the marriage relationship, yet marriage is not the only idea here. Camping together on cold nights and holding each other close for warmth, in the ancient world of Solomon's day, was a common practice. This comparison speaks to us of having a close personal and emotional connection with another person. We all can benefit from another person to warm our spirits and pick us up when we are down.

- Your friend can stand with you when an evil person or spirit assails you.

In Genesis 2:18, in the beginning of creation, when God placed Adam in the Garden of Eden, God declared, "It is not good for man to be alone." So, Eve was formed from Adam's side. As Bridges stated in *A Commentary on Ecclesiastes*, "If it was not good in Paradise, much less in the wilderness of the world." Simply put, man was made for relationships, fellowship, and communion with one another.

In the New Testament, the word used for "fellowship" is "koinonia," meaning communion, joint participation in something, intercourse, intimacy. As Christians, we are designed to provide a place of warmth, intimacy, and encouragement for one another. Without fellowship, we never grow and mature into the kind of individual God desires.

Acts 2:42 (NASB)

They were continually devoting themselves to the apostles' teaching and to fellowship, to the breaking of bread and to prayer.

1 John 1:7 (NASB)

but if we walk in the Light as He Himself is in the Light, we have fellowship with one another, and the blood of Jesus His Son cleanses us from all sin.

My description of the truth, "Two are better than one," comprises the aspects of true friendship. As Proverbs 18:24 states, a "true friend" sticks even closer to you than a brother. They are always there for you in both your good times and bad times, they see you at your best and worst, and still love and support you, whatever happens. This verse, of course, alludes to what our ultimate friendship with the Father should be, which is the most vital friendship or fellowship we can have. Even as Adam walked in the cool of the garden and communed daily with the Father, we can also enjoy such fellowship.

1 John 1:3 (NASB)

what we have seen and heard we proclaim to you also, so that you too may have fellowship with us; and indeed our fellowship is with the Father, and with His Son Jesus Christ.

We were made primarily for communion and intimacy with the Father in heaven, and flowing from that intercourse, God meant for us to join with others in relationship where together "two are better than one."

SIGNIFICANCE:

From the moment God created Adam and placed him in the Garden of Eden to take care of it, we can see Man was designed to have relationship and communion with others. God certainly realized this when He put Adam asleep and created Eve from Adam's side as a "help-meet" for Adam. The word that the Hebrew language conveys for "help-meet" means to succor or give comfort to another, which we know to be a vital function of friendship. We can also recognize the beautiful dynamics of the relationship between Adam and Eve with The Heavenly Father until sin separated them. They were strolling daily in the garden, having conversations with the Him.

Don't walk this life alone! Open yourself up, reach out to others and cultivate friendships, both with people and God. He made you for that!

8

A Fool's Folly or a Dreamer's Dream

Ecclesiastes 5:1-3

Guard your steps as you go to the house of God and draw near to listen rather than to offer the sacrifice of fools; for they do not know they are doing evil. Do not be hasty in word or impulsive in thought to bring up a matter in the presence of God. For God is in heaven and you are on the earth; therefore let your words be few. For the dream comes through much effort and

the voice of a fool through many words.

Today I want to look at the contrast in this passage between a "fool" and a "dreamer." It is as if Solomon is offering us a choice as to which way we will choose to live our lives. The Word of God has much to say about the "fool;" the word appears 56 times in the King James Version of the Bible! Of these, 48 of them are in the Old Testament and eight in the New Testament. Most of the Old Testament references are in the wisdom books of Psalms, Proverbs, and Ecclesiastes, but primarily in the book of Proverbs (32 occurrences). The most familiar is Psalms 14:1, which states that the one who says in his heart, "There is no God" is a fool. The real definition of a fool, as stated here, is rooted in a denial of God.

The most common word in the Old Testament in Hebrew for "fool" is kecyil (kes-el), meaning one who is stupid, dull of understanding, a simpleton, one who is arrogant. I think the real root idea of acting foolishly or being a fool stems from pride and arrogance. A fool always believes they know better than anyone else; they are a "know-it-all" with no need for advice or instruction. This concept is well supported in the wisdom books, especially in Proverbs, which was also written by Solomon.

Proverbs 11:29 (KJV)

He that troubleth his own house shall inherit the wind: and the fool shall be servant to the wise of heart.

Proverbs 12:15 (KJV)

The way of the fool is right in his own eyes: but he that hearkeneth unto counsel is wise.

Proverbs 14:16 (KJV)

A wise man feareth, and departeth from evil:
but the fool rageth and is confident.

Because a "fool" believes he has no need for advice or instruction from anyone, he has no obligation to acknowledge and seek counsel from a Creator that knows more than he does, as to him, no such Being exists. Being a fool is the supreme definition of arrogance and pride.

In Ecclesiastes 5:1-3, we are cautioned when we enter God's house about "not offering the sacrifice of fools," but rather to make sure we are careful with the words we choose, as well as the number of words we offer up to God. In other terms, do not babble on in disrespect before God and in His assembly as a "know-it-all" (what a fool would do), but rather humble yourself and be more sensitive to "draw near to listen."

This lesson brings us to the next idea of this passage, "The dream." I believe each person placed upon this planet has been given a natural ability to dream and make their dream into reality. Most of us have heard the phrase, "Don't just talk the talk, but walk the walk." A fool's way of doing things is to do much talking and bragging with little, if any, results. A real dream, which in this passage could either mean spiritual (one that God has given us), or something we ourselves come up with and then ask God to sanction and bless, takes real effort and work.

Ecclesiastes 5:3 (AMPC)

For a dream comes with much business and painful effort,

Ecclesiastes 5:3 (HCSB)

For dreams result from much work,

In this last phrase, when Solomon talks about the dream being realized through much business, a better rendering could be the dream comes through much travail.

Birthing a dream and bringing it forth into reality is much like the birth of a child. It takes real work and often much pain before that child is alive and thriving.

We must not be like the fool, feeling we need no one on our journey because we know best, but instead, we must be still and listen for the voice of God to instill within us a worthy vision. We then allow Him to strengthen and guide us to that dream's reality.

Proverbs 3:5-7

Lean on, trust in, and be confident in the Lord with all your heart and mind and do not rely on your own insight or understanding. In all your ways know, recognize, and acknowledge Him, and He will direct and make straight and plain your paths. Be not wise in your own eyes; reverently fear and worship the Lord and turn [entirely] away from evil.

Psalm 37:3-6 (AMPC)

Trust (lean on, rely on, and be confident) in the Lord and do good; so shall you dwell in the land and feed surely on His faithfulness, and truly you shall be fed. Delight yourself also in the Lord, and He will give you the desires and secret petitions of your heart. Commit your way to the Lord [roll and repose each care of your load on Him]; trust (lean on, rely on, and be confident) also in Him and He will bring it to pass. And He will make your uprightness and right standing with God go forth as the light, and your justice and right as [the shining sun of] the noonday.

SIGNIFICANCE:

Do not live your life as one that feels they know everything and has everything figured out. Choose the "work" of birthing a dream. Ask God for direction, and ask those wiser than you for help to make your dream a reality.

9

What's the Use In Living?

Ecclesiastes 6:12 (NLT)

In the few days of our meaningless lives, who knows how our days can best be spent? Our lives are like a shadow. Who can tell what will happen on this earth after we are gone?

In Chapter 6 of Ecclesiastes, the Searcher reaches a climax in his quest for the significance of life. He has spent an unlimited amount of money, tried endless pleasures and experiences, and accomplished many times over what an average man could ever accomplish in multiple lifetimes. And yet to him, it is like grasping at the air to obtain something that has lasting and tangible meaning.

We read at least four times in this chapter of the emptiness or meaninglessness that Solomon observes or experiences.

Verse 2: He sees a man who has obtained surpassing wealth and honor in his life, only to die passing it on to another to enjoy as "God has not given him the power or capacity to enjoy them...this is meaninglessness" (AMPC).

Verses 3-4: He laments that another man may have hundreds of children, and he dies as a poor man without enjoying the good things of life or even a decent burial. He may as well have ended up dead at birth to live such an existence. This, too, Solomon says is coming into the world in meaninglessness.

Verses 7-9: Attempting to feed and clothe yourself and take care of one's family: both rich and poor must do this, both wise and unwise do this as well. Daydreaming about something more; a better life also is meaninglessness.

Verses 10-12: Solomon says we already know most things that exist and their names and functions, so it is meaningless information for there is one above it all, namely God.

So at the end of the chapter in verse 12, the Searcher wonders just what use is there in living since all we do ends up meaningless, from his viewpoint.

I had mentioned earlier that the Hebrew word for "vanity" or "vain" that the KJV uses throughout Ecclesiastes is "hebel," meaning not only "meaninglessness," but is also from a root word meaning "vapor" or "breath." All these experiences Solomon mentions were like a breath or vapor in importance because they came and passed on so fast, like our very own breath. It's as if the Searcher is exclaiming, "How can there be any use in the activities of life? Men are born and pass on in such a relatively short time that any good they did is soon forgotten!"

The Apostle James puts it this way:

James 4:13-14

Come now, you who say, "Today or tomorrow we will go to such and such a city, and spend a year there and engage in business and make a profit." Yet you do not know what your life will be like tomorrow. You are just a vapor that appears for a little while and then vanishes away.

The predominant theme in the entire book of Ecclesiastes is to reveal to us the readers, just as the Searcher says, that life under the sun is meaningless, a worthless existence of going through the motions of day-to-day living that seem to take forever, yet in actuality pass us by in a blur. I believe God included this intriguing book to stir up a question in all of us where we each reach the end of ourselves, asking, "What's the use in living?" Ultimately, if we are honest--no other choice remains than to either say, "There is a God who made me for a reason and a purpose," or, as Solomon coveys from all his searching thus far, "There is no hope. We all die. And that's the end of the story." Solomon proposes if we all die, and that is the end of the story, then life has been nothing but a cruel lie.

I will close today's devotional with a brief message Paul preached in Athens on Mars Hill. Athens was called the University of Greece, and at one time had been the center of philosophy in the known world with men like Plato and Aristotle teaching there. In Paul's day, men still met to discuss the issues of life, and so here we find Paul, his spirit stirring within (Acts 17:16) at the multitude of idols that he saw on display that he knew people were worshipping out of confusion. We even know that they had created an altar to an UNKNOWN GOD (Acts 17:23).

Acts 17:23-28 (NLT)

for as I was walking along I saw your many shrines. And one of your altars had this inscription on it: 'To an Unknown God.' This God, whom you worship without knowing, is the one I'm telling you about. "He is the God who made the world and everything in it. Since he is Lord of heaven and earth, he doesn't live in man-made temples, and human hands can't serve his needs—for he has no needs. He himself gives life and breath to everything, and he satisfies every need.From one man] he created all the nations throughout the whole earth. He decided beforehand when they should rise and fall, and he determined their boundaries. "His purpose was for the nations to seek after God and perhaps feel their way toward him and find him—though he is not far from any one of us. For in him we live and move and exist. As some of your own poets have said, 'We are his offspring.'

In this story related to one of Paul's missionary journeys, we find a nation so confused they are worshipping thousands of gods, even to the extent of an "unknown god," so as not to miss out on the correct "god." The point is men tend to go from one extreme (that of no belief in any gods and a meaningless existence) to attempting to worship "something." In the end, as Paul states, "In Him we live and move and exist …" (Acts 17:28). Solomon realizes all men were created to worship. The question is What or Who will we worship? Some choose sports icons or Hollywood stars, others their spouse, and yet others worship possessions and riches.

In the end, one cannot deny that all men and women worship. We see the very proof of that every day through T.V. and the many social networks. Mankind has tried to assuage the need for adoration and honor by worshipping riches and possessions, which they can never take with them when their lives end, or by worshipping people, who are finite and will pass away only to be distant memories. God placed within each person the knowledge of His existence and that we were made for Him; this can be the only conclusion we come to if we are honest with ourselves.

SIGNIFICANCE:

Most people live their lives going through all the motions of life as if they were in a maze that they are never able to solve. Ecclesiastes slaps us in the face to wake us up to the reality that there is no other choice but to admit there is a God who has created us to live for and worship Him.

Isaiah 43:15

"I am the LORD, your Holy One, The Creator of Israel, your King"

Selah.

10

Perfume

Ecclesiastes 7:1

*A good name is better than
precious perfume...*

Perfume was probably first created in ancient Egypt. Our word perfume comes from the Latin word "per-fumus," meaning "through smoke," the smoke referring to incense. So, in its basest form, perfume was first created by combining incense with various oils from plants or trees like olive trees.

Perfume was used to provide pleasant scents when applied to one's body. People also used it to freshen up garments (Psalm 45:8), as well as the bedchamber (Proverbs 7:17). Perfume was a precious commodity in Bible times, most likely, because the people could not shower or bathe as frequently as we can today. It was even used in worship services in the temple (Exodus 30:22-28).

Ecclesiastes 7:1 is the first in a series of several proverbs showing that good things can come out of seemingly bad situations (adversity Ecclesiastes 7:14). This opening phrase is a beautiful play on words. The Hebrew word for name is "shem," and the Hebrew word for ointment or perfume is "shemen." The Searcher is saying that a good shem is better than precious shemen. This contrast, of course, is referring to perfume, which has the ability to attract others.

A good name carries influence with it; however, perfume, by comparison, does not. Fragrance, when applied or sprayed on an individual or garment, like the word "vapor" (hebel) used throughout Ecclesiastes, soon passes away. The scent of perfume may attract others for a time, but that attraction is soon gone. On the other hand, a respected NAME not only attracts others but endures.

In the world today, many are attempting to put on a sweet-smelling perfume or cologne that will make them appear or smell good to others, yet without a genuine, authentic identity (name), that soon fades away.

In conclusion, let's consider an account from the New Testament of a woman and an alabaster box of perfume.

Shortly before Jesus was to go to the cross, He went to visit His friends Mary, Martha, and Lazarus in Bethany. He met them for dinner and fellowship at the house of Simon the leper.

John 12:1-8 (NASB)

Jesus, therefore, six days before the Passover, came to Bethany where Lazarus was, whom Jesus had raised from the dead. So they made Him a supper there, and Martha was serving; but Lazarus was one of those reclining at the table with Him. Mary then took a pound of very *costly perfume of pure nard, and anointed the feet of Jesus and wiped His feet with her hair; and the house was filled with the fragrance of the perfume. But Judas Iscariot, one of His disciples, who was intending to betray Him, *said, "Why was this perfume not sold for three hundred denarii and given to poor people?" Now he said this, not because he was concerned about the poor, but because he was a thief, and as he had the money box, he used to pilfer what was put into it. Therefore Jesus said, "Let her alone, so that she may keep it for the day of My burial. For you always have the poor with you, but you do not always have Me."*

Here we see the life-long friends of Jesus, sisters Mary and Martha, and their brother Lazarus, who Jesus raised from the dead. Likely, this was the last time they were to see him alive, and here we are provided with a story that shows exquisite adoration, worship, and commitment to Jesus. John tells us Mary took a pound of very costly perfume of pure nard, and anointed the feet of Jesus and wiped His feet with her hair; the house filled with the aroma of the perfume.

The significance of this simple act leaves me in awe as I read through it. Here was a woman, Mary, who personally KNEW the King of Kings. She had seen Him raise her brother from the dead and certainly heard His proclamations of being the Messiah. With this act, she unashamedly acknowledged the essence of His purpose and ministry: the salvation and restoration of her people. By honoring Jesus and anointing Him for burial, she was showing that she KNEW the significance of HIS NAME:

John 11:25 (NIV)

Jesus said to her, "I am the resurrection and the

life. The one who believes in me will live, even
though they die."

John 8:58

*Jesus said to them, "Truly, truly, I say to you,
before Abraham was born, I am."*

John 8:12

*I am the light of the world. Whoever follows me
will never walk in darkness, but will have the
light of life.*

Mary declared the importance of Jesus' Name by
pouring costly perfume on Jesus' head and feet. Some
commentators say this perfume was worth a whole
year's salary! This demonstration shows total commitment, love, and worship for Jesus! Here was an aroma
that would not waft away because of what this very
personal act of adoration meant. In the book of Mark,
he said of this act of worship, "Wherever the gospel is
proclaimed in the whole world, what she has done will
be told in memory of her" (Mark 14:9). Because of this
simple act of worship, Mary's name would always be
remembered.

However, there is even more for us to ponder. The
flask Mary "broke" was a pure white Alabaster box
or container. Alabaster is a genuine white stone with
much the same appearance of marble. However, it is
easily etched or carved upon; it crumbles easily. We
are figuratively (typologically) vessels pouring out our
lives before the Father in worship.

2 Corinthians 4:7

*But we have this treasure in earthen vessels, so
that the surpassing greatness of the power will
be of God and not from ourselves;*

In verses 8-11, the scripture alludes to the process

of being broken through trials and afflictions. We are easily "broken" like the earthen vessel above made of pure white seashells, which easily crumbled or shattered.

2 Corinthians 4:8-11

we are afflicted in every way, but not crushed; perplexed, but not despairing; persecuted, but not forsaken; struck down, but not destroyed; always carrying about in the body the dying of Jesus, so that the life of Jesus also may be manifested in our body. For we who live are constantly being delivered over to death for Jesus' sake, so that the life of Jesus also may be manifested in our mortal flesh.

As this process of trial and adversity breaks us, the life of Jesus can exude out of us to others, which is a form of worship as we give ourselves to the world. It has been scientifically proven that we each as human beings carry a distinct body odor or "scent." We can also bring the sweet scent of His presence and Spirit that can waft out of us to draw others to the Father, just like when Mary's smell of perfume filled the whole room once she broke the flask. Song of Solomon 4:16 expresses the idea that the Father wants the fragrance of US, His garden, to carry everywhere.

Our individual scents, because of His Spirit within us, are precious to Him.

Revelation 8:4

And the smoke of the incense, with the prayers of the saints, went up before God out of the angel's hand

2 Corinthians 2:15

for we are a sweet fragrance of Christ to God among those who are being saved and among those who are perishing;

Ephesians 5:2

For we are a fragrance of Christ to God among those who are being saved and among those who are perishing;

SIGNIFICANCE:

We are HIS perfume. And because of the work Jesus accomplished, and because we are IN Him, our scent will carry on for eternity.

I Corinthians 1:30

But by His doing you are in Christ Jesus, who became to us wisdom from God, and righteousness and sanctification, and redemption,

11

Considering Adversity

Ecclesiastes 7:13-14 (Darby)

Consider the work of God; for who can make straight what He hath made crooked? In the day of prosperity enjoy the good, and in the day of adversity consider: God hath also set the one beside the other, to the end that man should find out nothing {of what shall be} after him.

My heart was greatly saddened and numb as I wrote this chapter. A macabre twist of fate that just as I had been preparing to write about "adversity," this past weekend, 31 people were left dead in our nation in two separate, cowardly and despicable mass shootings. The first took place in El Paso, Texas, and the next in Dayton, Ohio. These events are really beyond any words to express the grief, hopelessness, and anger we now feel as a nation.

So what thoughts or insights can I share to help bring healing in this painful season? Words seem so inadequate at a time like this. However, since we are staring straight in the face of such a terrible event, perhaps it is also the time and season to take to heart the Searcher's admonition to "Consider the Day of Adversity."

In these two verses, the word "consider" is mentioned twice. We must consider the work of God and consider that God has made both days of prosperity and days of adversity. Solomon connects adversity and crookedness as being the same and involving God's work. The wise counselor here feels that it is so important to "consider adversity" that he admonishes us twice to stop and take a closer look at adversity. He asks us to take time to contemplate the elements and ramifications of the experience of ADVERSITY.

In our present world, this tragic event of the merciless killing of so many may be discussed for, maybe a few weeks or so, and then, like so many other times, forgotten, as the majority of people mindlessly go on living, leaving the families affected to try and attempt to put their shattered lives back together again. In Hebrew, the word "CONSIDER" is better rendered to "stop, pause, meditate on, give attention to." In other words, do not be so quick just to move on. Rather, give adversity some serious thought to see what can be learned from that situation to benefit us in the future.

The very first thing that I want to get across to you, the reader, is that GOD DID NOT CAUSE THIS devastating shooting! This passage in Ecclesiastes does look like he is saying that God makes things crooked and has created, or set aside, a day of adversity for men, and yet throughout the Bible, God's defining traits are love and goodness.

Psalm 145:9

The LORD is good to all, And His mercies are over all His works.

Psalm 86:5

For You, Lord, are good, and ready to forgive, And abundant in loving-kindness to all who call upon You.

I Chronicles 16:34

O give thanks to the LORD, for He is good; For His lovingkindness is everlasting.

1 John 4:9-11 (ESV)

In this the love of God was made manifest among us, that God sent his only Son into the world so that we might live through him. In this is love, not that we have loved God but that he loved us and sent his Son to be the propitiation for our sins. Beloved, if God so loved us, we also ought to love one another.

There is an answer to this apparent contradiction concerning God's character of goodness and love versus a God that causes us adversity and trouble. The simple answer is that by sinning and eating of the tree of the knowledge of good and evil in the Garden of Eden, Adam and Eve chose their own wisdom and mind above God's best. From that day forward, sin, adversity, and crookedness entered the world in which we live.

How has God made situations and events crooked? Not by Himself DOING those acts, but by allowing man a choice and thus he, at times, chooses despicable things and faces adverse situations due to the world's fall after creation. Man now must work and earn his way by the sweat of his labor. He must contend with weeds, sickness, the car breaking, the baby being sick, loved ones passing on, and sadly, mass murder. This is an imperfect world.

My next thought then is to ask how each of us will personally deal with ADVERSITY when it comes our way, and it will come our way, as Jesus said, "He sends His rain on the just and the unjust alike" (Matthew 5:45 NLT).

First, let's look at the meaning of ADVERSITY and allow that to saturate our minds and hearts.

In Hebrew, the word is "ra" and has these following connotations: affliction, calamity, distress, hurt, evil, sorrow, trouble, being mistreated. Adversity is not only physical duress but often accompanies a heavy mental and emotional state of being as well. The word "ra" comes from a root word meaning to spoil, harm, break, or grind into pieces that are good for nothing--worthless!

Have you ever felt in your life that you had reached a point of being worthless, or good for nothing because of all the adversity that assailed you? I am most certain Job felt that way also, as we read in Job Chapter 1 that he basically lost all his wealth and children. His response in all this calamity?

Job 1:20

Then Job arose and tore his robe and shaved his head, and he fell to the ground and worshiped.

The next adversity he faced was to have his entire body racked with pain as satan was allowed to afflict his body with terrible boils.

Job 2:9

At this point his wife threw up her hands and exclaimed, "Do you still hold fast your integrity? Curse God and die!"

And yet Job's response was,

Job 2:10a

...You speak as one of the foolish women speaks. Shall we indeed accept good from God and not accept adversity?"

This response was almost a quote of our verse today in Ecclesiastes: to accept adversity from God as there is something we might learn in the test. In the end, Job did NOT sin! What a testimony of faith and trust in God! In Chapter 1 of Job, it is said of him, "That man was blameless, upright, fearing God and turning away from evil" (Job 1:1).

There are many lessons to be learned from ADVERSITY:

- To pay attention to the Father (Psalm 119:67, 71)

- There are many afflictions in life yet God helps us (John 16:33)

- We are called as sons and daughters to embrace suffering (Philippians 3:10)

- The Father uses chastisement as our earthly fathers do to demonstrate His love for us (Hebrews 12:5-12)

- Suffering prepares us to enter God's Kingdom (Acts 14:22)

- The Father TESTS our faith, just as we are tested in school, to see if we are ready to move higher in Him. (I Peter 1:5-7, Job 23:10)

Unless one is willing to accept the GIFT that Adversity brings, there can be no exaltation.

I Peter 5:6-10

Therefore humble yourselves under the mighty hand of God, that He may exalt you at the proper time, casting all your anxiety on Him, because He cares for you. Be of sober spirit, be on the alert. Your adversary, the devil, prowls around like a roaring lion, seeking someone to devour. But resist him, firm in your faith, knowing that the same experiences of suffering are being accomplished by your brethren who are in the world. After you have suffered for a little while, the God of all grace, who called you to His eternal glory in Christ, will Himself perfect, confirm, strengthen and establish you.

To truly accept the GIFT adversity brings means that we must be willing to humble ourselves before God, admitting we can never figure everything out on our own. It is only then that we will see and understand all that God has for us, and as Paul said, we must realize He is able to do far more abundantly and beyond all that we could ever ask or think (Ephesians 3:20). We must repent, or learn to have a different mindset, about the trials, testing, and afflictions that come our way since we are still being perfected while living in an imperfect world.

As James also tells us in Chapter 1, we must learn to "count it all joy," or as The English Bible scholar and translator J.B Phillips renders this phrase, "welcome that trial of adversity" into our lives as if we were welcoming home a long lost relative. We can now realize the true gift of adversity is patience and perfection of character being molded into our lives.

In Matthew 5:3, Jesus taught that those who were

poor or beggarly, or truly needy in spirit, would have the Kingdom of God rewarded to them in all its joy and fullness. We can only see and possess all the blessings and rewards God has for us by using the gift adversity brings to cause us to come to God and admit our need of Him to be the Lord of our lives.

When David prayed his sobering prayer of repentance from sin with Bathsheba in Psalm 51:17, he pleaded with God to have a BROKEN spirit and a BROKEN and CONTRITE heart. In the Hebrew language, both BROKEN and CONTRITE in their root forms mean to be shattered and ground up into pieces beyond recognition. This prayer shows then that David had accepted the "Gift of Adversity" that God had set before him. Amazingly this takes us back to the underlying root meaning of ADVERSITY, which also means to be broken and ground up into nothing. Another idea that we can also consider here is that David ended up in this place of desperate repentance because of willful sin. He saw Bathsheba one day when she was on her deck bathing, he began to entertain a desire for her, he then acted on that sinful desire, took her for his own, and had sexual relations with her. This decision resulted in her becoming pregnant with his child. He then, for some months, began to attempt to cover up this sin. David even went so far as even to have her husband Uriah killed by placing him at the front of a battle line. Now he was also guilty of murder! The Apostle James addresses this problem well in the New Testament about just how destructive sinful adversity can be if allowed to continue.

James 1:15-16

Then when lust has conceived, it gives birth to sin; and when sin is accomplished, it brings forth death. Do not be deceived, my beloved brethren.

What a fantastic example this shows us of the love and grace of our Heavenly Father for us! Even when we may commit acts of sin that are as serious as what David did and can seem beyond forgiveness or repair, we can, as I like to say, "Throw gas on my fire of sin." We do something wrong and then accelerate a negative situation through attempting to fix it by covering it up, just as David did. All this "self-help" only brings more Adversity upon us and even those around us, by our own sinful acts that we chose. We could call this "Self-Inflicted Adversity!" Even in the direst circumstances that our own hands created, the Heavenly Father is just waiting for us to turn, BACK TO HIM! (See Romans 8:28, Luke 15:11-24). Adversity, whether it comes into our lives through the circumstances of life beyond our control or through our own wayward actions of sin, is all about leading us to fully humble ourselves in repentance, submission, and trust in our Heavenly Father.

We must realize that only by trusting in Him can we have the life He desires for us.

SIGNIFICANCE:

We must be willing to accept the "Gift of Adversity," or we may miss some fundamental direction and transformation God has planned for us.

So, when all kinds of adversity in life assail you, will you "CONSIDER the work of God" that He is creating in you?

12

Who Is Like A Wise Man?

Ecclesiastes 8:1

Who is like the wise man and who knows the interpretation of a matter? A man's wisdom illumines him and causes his stern face to beam.

This short passage shows us a powerful, four-fold picture of the transformation that takes place when a person discovers the true wisdom of righteousness that God provides as a gift to those who walk uprightly with Him and fear Him. This wisdom is defined well by the Apostle James,

James 3:13,17

"Who among you is wise and understanding?

> *Let him show by his good behavior his deeds*
> *in the gentleness of wisdom... But the wisdom*
> *from above is first pure, then peaceable, gentle,*
> *reasonable, full of mercy and good fruits, un-*
> *wavering, without hypocrisy."*

The first thing wisdom accomplishes in us is to reveal who we are as unique sons and daughters of the Father. "Who among you is wise?" In the culture of our world today, so many are trying to be someone they are not. We are bombarded daily on the internet, TV, radio, etc. to look like, dress like, or talk like some popular movie or sports star. However, the wonderful and freeing message is that when you know Christ, you are a new creation, unique, and made beautiful in Him.

2 Corinthians 5:17 (CSB)

Therefore, if anyone is in Christ, he is a new
creation; the old has passed away, and see, the
new has come!

You will have become an original son or daughter birthed by the Spirit of God.

Secondly, you will be given godly wisdom that will unlock secret knowledge, "who knows the interpretation of a matter?" Just as God gave Solomon more wisdom than any other person in the world, and everyone sought him out for answers on numerous issues (1 Kings 4:29-34, 1 Kings 10), God desires to raise up "Prophetic Solomons" to provide solutions to problems we face in this world today. This is wisdom that will cause such wonder and astonishment that people will turn to the Father. In 1 Corinthians 2:15-16, Paul states, "He who is spiritual appraises (judges) ALL Things." Why? Because, as the next verse says, "We have the mind of Christ," who is better than the sons and daughters of

God to provide solutions in this confusing world?

Thirdly, a person who has received the wisdom from above that is first pure, then peaceable, gentle, reasonable, full of mercy and good fruits, cannot help but experience visible joy. The NASB translation says wisdom "causes his stern face to beam." This is the work of God's grace that gives us hope when we truly fear and reverence God in our lives, knowing that He has all things under His control.

Proverbs 3:13 (KJV)

Happy is the man that findeth wisdom, and the man that getteth understanding.

Psalms 111:10 (KJV)

The fear of the Lord is the beginning of wisdom.

Finally, the beaming and joyful face that is a result of discovering God's wisdom changes a person's whole disposition and countenance, His whole being as it were. Because his trust and confidence are in God, he can now hold his head up high without shame!

Psalms 34:5

They looked to Him and were radiant, And their faces will never be ashamed...

SIGNIFICANCE:

Wisdom then provides for us a unique identity in the Father, giving us confidence that we can supply answers for others in their lives. This, in turn, will produce within us joy and the peace and satisfaction that are the true essence of Godly wisdom.

13

Living Life To The Fullest In The Power of God

Ecclesiastes 9:7-11

Go then, eat your bread in happiness and drink your wine with a cheerful heart; for God has already approved your works. Let your clothes be white all the time, and let not oil be lacking on your head. Enjoy life with the woman whom you love all the days of your fleeting life which He has given to you under the sun; for this is your reward in life and in your toil in which you have labored under the sun. Whatever your hand finds to do, do it with all your might; for there is no activity or planning or knowledge or wisdom in Sheol where you are going. I again saw under the sun that the race is not to the swift and the battle is not to the warriors, and neither is bread to the wise nor wealth to the discerning nor favor to men of ability; for time and chance overtake them all.

We now come to a passage about midway through Chapter 9 that is my favorite passage in the whole book of Ecclesiastes. These five verses (Ecc. 9:7-11) caught my eye years ago when I first began to study this book so intensely. After hours of research and study of these verses, I wrote my own version of the text based on the original language, context, commentaries, and what I felt was the Searcher's meaning. I will now share it with you and then conclude with some notable observations.

Ecclesiastes 9:7-11 (M.P.G. - Author's translation)

Go thy way living your life freely. Eat your bread and drink your wine with a joyful and celebratory heart as the Father has already paid your debt in full and is overjoyed with what you have accomplished. Let your clothing always be spotless and pure and continue daily to walk in the fullness of my Spirit. Live blissfully with your spouse loving them con-

siderately all the days of your earthly life that swiftly passes by, for this will be your reward for all your labors in this brief life. Whatever you do in this temporary earthly existence do it with all your might and passion, holding nothing back! (for once you die there are no more opportunities).

Always remember apart from the Heavenly Father you will never find fulfillment, security, and happiness in this world. Also, keep in mind that natural abilities do not always win the day. You will encounter many uncertainties, perplexities, temptations, and hardships, therefore, tap into My grace and power to sustain you along the way in your journey through this temporary existence on earth.

What impacted my heart so much when I read this passage is catching a glimpse of the New Testament Covenant hidden within this text. My grandfather taught me a principle as a young lad that has served me well in studying the Word of God. He was a traveling preacher, and we often discussed the power and wonder of God's Word together. Sometimes He would use this saying in speaking about God's truth hidden from a casual observer. "The New is in the Old concealed, and the Old is in the New revealed." What this means is many of God's truths in the Old Testament are "hidden" from a casual observer. Many of the accounts in the Old Testament and what they spoke of had hidden and symbolic meaning waiting to be discovered by those who were hungry for God's Truth.

Matthew 5:6

"Blessed are those who hunger and thirst for righteousness, for they shall be satisfied."

The other part of this saying means that for those fortunate enough to see the symbols of deeper truths in the Old Testament will know they are to be interpreted by the New Testament ("The Old is in the New revealed"). The reality is the Old Testament was the Old Covenant made between God and man, and when Jesus died on the cross for the sins of mankind, tearing the veil in the temple from top to bottom, the New Covenant was ushered in.

Matthew 27:50-51

And Jesus cried out again with a loud voice, and yielded up His spirit. And behold, the veil of the temple was torn in two from top to bottom; and the earth shook and the rocks were split.

Here is the beauty that captured my eyes as I read the verses that Solomon penned in this chapter: I was seeing the HOPE of the New Covenant, not easily recognized. Amazingly, in the midst of all of Solomon's frustrated, often negative search for the meaning of life, God sheds a bit of light back into Solomon's darkened heart that Solomon must have seen to write these words in the manner in which he does.

Look at these phrases once again, "God has already approved your works," "Let your clothes be white all the time," "let not oil be lacking on your head."

Or as I translated, "the Father has already paid your debt in full," "Let your clothing always be spotless and pure," "Continue to daily walk in the fullness of my spirit,"

These are surely references to the New Covenant Jesus established and empowered us to walk in when He died on the cross, shedding His blood for our sins.

Consider the following New Testament verses that interpret what Solomon expressed here in Ecclesiastes.

He paid for our sin:

Mark 10:45

For even the Son of Man did not come to be served, but to serve, and to give His life a ransom for many.

Ephesians 1:7

In Him we have redemption through His blood, the forgiveness of our trespasses, according to the riches of His grace

As His Church, we are to be pure and spotless:

Ephesians 5:27

that He might present to Himself the church in all her glory, having no spot or wrinkle or any such thing; but that she would be holy and blameless.

1 John 3:3

And everyone who has this hope fixed on Him purifies himself, just as He is pure.

We are to be filled with and walking in His Spirit:

Ephesians 5:18

And do not get drunk with wine, for that is dissipation, but be filled with the Spirit,

Galatians 5:16

But I say, walk by the Spirit, and you will not carry out the desire of the flesh.

SIGNIFICANCE:

When we are born-again, spirit-filled Saints, walking fully-empowered by God through this life, we can fully enjoy our lives. We can experience all the created pleasures of life, such as fine food, family life, our careers, and many other delights God has made for us in His creation. It does not matter if everything turns out perfectly. We will have hardships and even fail at times, yet we know as His Sons and Daughters we are accepted by Him, and one day we will spend all of eternity with Him in joy, peace, and love beyond any explanation. We can truly live and enjoy this short life to the FULLEST in HIS Power!

14

Some Proverbs For Living

Ecclesiastes 10:1,8,10

Dead flies make the perfumer's ointment give off a stench; so a little folly outweighs wisdom and honor. ... He who digs a pit will fall into it, and a serpent will bite him who breaks through a wall If the iron is blunt, and one does not sharpen the edge, he must use more strength, but wisdom helps one to succeed.

For today's devotion, I want us to consider several proverbs of wisdom by Solomon in Ecclesiastes that can help us live in this often complex and uncertain world. Though they were written over 2900 years ago in another time and culture, the precepts he so wisely shared are still applicable for us today.

Solomon is better known for writing the majority of the Book of Proverbs in the earlier part of his reign as King when he led Israel to be the most prosperous nation in the world. Perhaps many of these short adages of wisdom were penned from experiences he had with other nations' leaders like the Queen of Sheeba who "came to prove him with hard questions" (1 Kings 10:1).

A proverb is simply a short, pithy saying expressing a truth about human behavior. Solomon used them well to evaluate humans' actions and their consequences. Besides being short and to the point, these thoughtful axioms often used figurative language along with, at times, making two opposite points for effect--usually, a negative thought contrasted with a positive view.

Having said all of that, let's now look at some of these simple sayings he was inspired to pen in Ecclesiastes 10 and see if we can decipher how they might best apply to our lives today.

Ecclesiastes 10:1

Dead flies make a perfumer's oil stink, so a little foolishness is weightier than wisdom and honor.

This scripture is such a powerful word of advice, that if we can assimilate it early as young adults or even youngsters, it can save us much pain and anguish as we live day-to-day. Simply stated, if you have the most expensive and wonderfully scented perfume in all the land and even a very tiny fly or insect we can hardly see penetrates the bottle, that perfume is ruined and now worthless. Likewise, in life and business, if you have built up and displayed a strong, integral character of being forthright, honest, and genuine, even a slight, detrimental act can irreparably damage or ruin that character overnight. It often takes years to build a reputable business in a community, or virtuous character, and yet sadly, one ill-thought-out act can bring that all down in a moment. How many of us have heard in the media of trusted companies making an error in customer service or employee relations? Or closer to home, we have heard of pastors and religious leaders who preached wonderful, life-changing messages and were pillars of stability in their communities, falling in an act of lustful passion or dishonest conduct. Those once viewed with impeccable character, sadly, in this life are usually forever tainted, and no longer have the positive influence God intended.

Ecclesiastes 10:8

He who digs a pit may fall into it, and a serpent may bite him who breaks through a wall.

Here, the menial task of digging ditches or a deep hole and excavating old building structures is mentioned to share some truths with us about common human behaviors we are all challenged with at times in our lives. Digging a ditch or demolishing old walls from buildings could be dangerous physically to us, and yet the Searcher is using symbolism here to show attitudes and acts that could be spiritually damaging and dangerous for us. In the metaphor that Solomon alludes to here, "digging a ditch" would be purposely setting up a circumstance or situation to hurt someone or get even with them for a perceived wrong they have done to you. For example, have you ever had a friend or loved one you were close to for a long time, that was a confidant to you, turn on you and do something terribly wrong to you? They abandon you and even speak defamatory lies about you. Well, human nature is to want to get even or at least entertain that idea in our minds. In this wise adage, Solomon is saying if you actually go "lay a trap (dig a ditch)" for this person to make them look bad, injure them, or to get even in some way, you yourself may fall into that trap hurting and injuring yourself. Reading this proverb, I am reminded of the TV show *48 Hours* that my wife and I watch from time to time, which is often about a spouse or loved one who is murdered by the other spouse. The impetus is usually bitterness over situations like custody of children, money, or just a relationship gone wrong in which one party feels betrayed by the other. The spouse who "got even" through murder ends up in prison. We must give these hurts to the Father, and as hard as it may be, forgive them and save ourselves much pain.

Romans 12:17-19

Never pay back evil for evil to anyone. Respect what is right in the sight of all men. If possible, so far as it depends on you, be at peace with all men. Never take your own revenge, beloved, but leave room for the wrath of God, for it is written, "Vengeance is Mine, I will repay, says the Lord."

Another lesson is that a wise person understands that attempting to break down or demolish a "wall" of obstruction to get at someone or something that wronged you may end up poisoning you instead. Also, for me, I have found out the hard way attempting to force someone to forgive me when I have wronged them, just to relieve my conscience, never works. You can not force another to forgive you; trying to break down someone's resistance to me only made me angrier and triggered a serpent from within that bit me mentally and emotionally.

Ecclesiastes 10:10

If the axe is dull and he does not sharpen its

edge, then he must exert more strength. Wisdom has the advantage of success.

This is one of my favorite proverbs. Solomon alludes to a woodsman in the woods, chopping down trees. It is easy to understand: if the woodsman did not take time to sharpen his axe before he begins the task of chopping wood, it would take him much longer to do this job with a dull axe. How often are we like that woodsman rushing out to get the job done, and because we did not take time and effort to prepare beforehand (sharpen the axe), that job takes much longer than anticipated?

We rush out not being equipped, and instead of saving time and even doing a good job with the task at hand, we take much longer. Even worse, we sometimes make a bungled mess, which in turn takes even more time to resolve. Note again what Solomon says, "Wisdom has the advantage of success." A wise person is prepared for the work that life brings our way. Wisdom will save us time, energy, stress, and, most likely, the chance of making costly mistakes. One definition of wisdom is "a proper application of knowledge." Do not be like I have tended to be over the years and rush ahead, thinking I will save time attempting to put the kid's bike or the new barbeque together without FIRST reading the directions. I guarantee you, more often than not, you will end up with a screwed-up mess, costing more time, if you do not pause to read the directions first.

Luke 14:28-30

For which one of you, when he wants to build a tower, does not first sit down and calculate the cost to see if he has enough to complete it? Otherwise, when he has laid a foundation and is not able to finish, all who observe it begin to ridicule him, saying, "This man began to build and was not able to finish."

SIGNIFICANCE:

The Proverbs were written by Solomon, who was inspired by God, to give us simple and practical principles to help us live this life in better and more efficient ways. So today, watch what you say to others on the job or in your community; people are taking notice of you and how you conduct yourself. Jesus said offenses would come, so be careful to guard your heart when others hurt you intentionally or not. And finally, work "smarter," not "harder," and you will save yourself much time and stress.

15

Cast Your Bread Upon The Waters

Ecclesiastes 11:1-6

Cast your bread on the surface of the waters, for you will find it after many days. Divide your portion to seven, or even to eight, for you do not know what misfortune may occur on the earth. If the clouds are full, they pour out rain upon the earth; and whether a tree falls toward the south or toward the north, wherever the tree falls, there it lies. He who watches

*the wind will not sow and he who looks at
the clouds will not reap. Just as you do not
know the path of the wind and how bones
are formed in the womb of the pregnant
woman, so you do not know the activity
of God who makes all things. Sow your
seed in the morning and do not be idle in
the evening, for you do not know whether
morning or evening sowing will succeed, or
whether both of them alike will be good.*

This is such a beautiful and RICH portion of Scripture! My heart is so FULL as I pen this devotional thought. There are special enlightenment and blessing that I pray for you to receive from what Solomon is sharing. Back in the mid-'90s, I spent three or four years studying Ecclesiastes and teaching a Wednesday night class on the book. The notes from back then that I have for these scriptures in Chapter 11 seem so inadequate to express how I have experienced this concept in my life in the last three years. Solomon is basically saying to throw out your sustenance to those in need around you, in a carefree, almost reckless manner! "Cast your Bread (your monies) upon the waters," that is, give out to the world and region you occupy from your means. "For in many days you will find it again," meaning that God will reward and bless you when you are in need.

Here the Searcher is expressing a heart-felt exhortation TO GIVE generously and then see what God will do! I cannot help but think of what Jesus said in Luke:

Luke 6:38
*Give, and it will be given to you. They will pour
into your lap a good measure—pressed down,*

shaken together, and running over. For by your standard of measure it will be measured to you in return.

"Cast your bread on the waters" was an idiom often used in Israel that characterized wasteful giving, and yet here, the Searcher is inspired to admonish us to give unreservedly. Sure, wisdom is needed in who we deliver to and possibly how much, however, God desires us to give, holding nothing back in fear! Sometimes we need to take a STEP of FAITH and GIVE, even sometimes to others when we naturally in our own rationale would not, like the beggar on the corner of your city street.

"Divide your portion to seven or eight..." Once again, here is another Hebrew idiom saying give to as many folks as you possibly can, and then some! Do not just stop with your tithe or giving to the Red Cross. When you know your neighbor is in need and without a job, or even when a stranger comes to your door, GIVE. When we are moved by God to give in this way, the Hebrew language implies we will be preventing evil from happening on the earth.

Also, have you ever considered that by giving in such a generous, unreserved way, you might be meeting many unexpressed needs as well? We may never know how significant our seemingly small amount of giving impacted others until we are in heaven.

Solomon continues this theme with four more reasons to give. He expresses this in four beautiful proverbs to drive his point home for us.

If the clouds are full, they pour out rain upon the earth...Verse 3.

The idea here is we as God's people should be so full of His love and Spirit that we will pour out blessings upon those around us. Jesus said it this way, "Freely you have received, freely give" (Matthew 10:8).

Also in Verse 3, when the Searcher speaks about trees falling in a forest, he is saying, "Wherever a tree falls, there it lies."

Here the meaning for us is, as the old saying goes, "Bloom where you are planted!" In other words, as sovereignly God controls where and when trees fall in each forest around the planet, so he is telling us to be a blessing in the region where we reside. Supply the needs of those in your community. Please note, in this internet day and age, your community may not be limited to just your geographic region, but God may join you with other brethren and people around our world. Just as He has done with me, He may put on your heart to support those near and far.

Our third reason for generously giving is found in verse 4: "He who watches the wind will not sow and he who looks at the clouds will not reap."

Wow! This is possibly the most critical principle Solomon expresses here. One of the greatest hindrances to all people today in all areas of their lives is PRO-CRASTINATION! I am reminded of a great quote I read from James Clear at JamesClear.com about this just yesterday:

"Life is short. And if life is short, then moving quickly matters. Launch the product. Write the book. Ask the question. Take the chance. Be thoughtful, but get moving."

In other words, do not wait for that perfect time in life to do different things, including giving to others. Don't wait to give until you have a lot saved up before giving. If you wait until all in your life is perfect, you will never give because things will never be perfect! Begin to step out and give as you are able. Ask God to guide you regarding who and how much to give, and He will show you those who could use your help. This particular meditation is not about tithing but speaks to giving beyond the tithe (which I consider to be a requirement from God for His sons and daughters). The Bible speaks of giving 10% of our income (I believe it to be gross income) in a tithe. Tithing takes FAITH that God will provide a way for you to do it because sometimes in life, it's not easy. God will provide if, in faith, you determine to tithe. That means setting aside the "TENTH" before using any of the other money you have been blessed with as income.

Finally, the fourth truth about generous giving is found in verses 5 and 6:

Just as you do not know the path of the wind and how bones are formed in the womb of the pregnant woman, so you do not know the activity of God who makes all things. Sow your seed in the morning and do not be idle in the evening, for you do not know whether morning or evening sowing will succeed, or whether both of them alike will be good.

Notice in both verses the phrase, "you do not know" is mentioned twice. Once again, Solomon speaks of mysteries "under the sun" beyond our comprehension apart from God; even in knowing Him, we are made to wonder! Even in our 21st century, we certainly do not fully comprehend "how life and spirit are formed in the bones of a pregnant woman."

How is a unique personality passed on through a forming, yet still an unborn fetus, which distinguishes man from just another animal? No one has that answer, but life is present; the baby (fetus) is a human being. So much for the abortion supporter saying the fetus is not living; this verse proves otherwise.

These verses point out our lack of understanding about how the power of God works in our universe. We do not know how He produces life or gives us gifts and uses them. As Paul said in Romans 11:33, "Oh, the depth of the riches both of the wisdom and knowledge of God! How unsearchable are His judgments and unfathomable His ways!"

Remember the account of Jesus watching folks throw money into the temple treasury box? One woman threw in two mites, or two pennies in our day. The mite was the lowest denomination in the Jewish culture, yet Jesus said of her, "This poor widow put in more than all of them" (Luke 21:3).

That is amazing! We look at that and ask just how can Jesus' math be correct as many gave far more than her that day?!

This is an amazing story that has been retold thousands of times all over the world. Just what did Jesus mean? What He said that day was the literal truth. This account has motivated more folks to give than any story told since. It is profoundly true that in God's power and wisdom, this tiny gift multiplied throughout the history of the Church. God's power causes us to use our gifts, however small and insignificant they may seem, for His glory. We may never know in our lives how God will use our monetary gifts, big or small, to have a life-changing impact on someone just at the time they need it.

Today God desires to raise up a group of generous and cheerful givers, as my friend Melissa VanSchaik would say, "To empower the Army of God to go forth in His plans and purposes to transform the world for Him." ("for God loves a cheerful giver." 2 Corinthians 9:7).

SIGNIFICANCE:

God will change and bless your life as well as many others' if you just "cast your bread upon the waters!"

16

Goads & Nails From The Good Shepherd

Ecclesiastes 12:11 (NIV)

The words of the wise are like goads, their collected sayings like firmly embedded nails-given by one shepherd.

As we come towards the end of this mysteriously intriguing book of Ecclesiastes, once again, we see a statement that can only point to another beautiful New Covenant Truth. The Searcher says wise words are like goads or embedded nails given by ONE SHEPHERD. Of course, the ONE Shepherd was the Son of God, Jesus Christ, revealed in the New Testament.

John 10:11-16

"I am the good shepherd; the good shepherd lays down His life for the sheep. He who is a hired hand, and not a shepherd, who is not the owner of the sheep, sees the wolf coming, and leaves the sheep and flees, and the wolf snatches them and scatters them. He flees because he is a hired hand and is not concerned about the sheep. I am the good shepherd, and I know My own and My own know Me, even as the Father knows Me and I know the Father; and I lay down My life for the sheep. I have other sheep, which are not of this fold; I must bring them also, and they will hear My voice; and they will become one flock with one shepherd.

1 Peter 5:4

And when the Chief Shepherd appears, you will receive the unfading crown of glory.

Isaiah 40:11

Like a shepherd He will tend His flock, In His arm He will gather the lambs and carry them in his bosom; He will gently lead the nursing ewes.

As His Sons and Daughters, we can be confident and at peace that "The ONE SHEPHERD," Jesus, who is called the GOOD Shepherd, will take care of us.

We can trust Jesus and the promises He has given us because He IS GOOD. Literally, He is the most precious, suitable, commendable, admirable, most excellent in character, most genuine, most morally excellent, comforting, and honest Person that ever lived.

SHEPHERD, again literally meaning, "as a good shepherd." He is a watcher, defender, healer, finder of the lost, and lover of our souls (all these meanings for GOOD and SHEPHERD are implied by the original languages of Hebrew and Greek in which the Old and New Testaments were written in, respectively).

So let's look for a moment at what the GOOD SHEPHERD is giving His Sheep.

First of all, "goads" are mentioned. A goad was a shepherd's stick or staff with spikes or nails in the side of it to prod or "goad along" sheep or cattle in the way they should go or to keep moving (1 Samuel 13:21 KJV). The goads were said to be wise words; here in this picture they refer to the wise words penned through Solomon to give admonishment and direction, but they can refer to the whole Word of God.

1 Corinthians 10:11

Now these things happened to them as an example, and they were written for our instruction, upon whom the ends of the ages have come...

Romans 15:4

For whatever was written in earlier times was written for our instruction, so that through perseverance and the encouragement of the Scriptures we might have hope.

("Instruction" is also translated "admonishment or admonition.")

In Acts 2, when Peter preached a sermon on Pentecost and the Holy Spirit fell, verses 37-38 say,

When they heard this, they were pierced to the heart, and said to Peter and the rest of the apostles, "Brethren, what shall we do?" Peter said to them, "Repent, and each of you be baptized in the name of Jesus Christ for the forgiveness of your sins; and you will receive the gift of the Holy Spirit."

This piercing of heart is a related word to being pricked or goaded. These individuals were "pierced, moved in heart or goaded" to respond to Peter's message and repent of their sin, be baptized, and receive the Holy Spirit.

In Psalms, David speaks of being "afflicted," or chastised, which is similar to being goaded.

Psalm 119:67

Before I was afflicted I went astray, But now I keep your word.

Psalm 119:71

It is good for me that I was afflicted, That I may learn your ways.

We all need to be goaded at times by the ONE Shepherd who loves us to keep us from sin, and to keep us moving in the right direction.

Finally, the Word of God ("collected sayings") are like "embedded nails" in that they keep us fixed, planted, and established (nailed down) in HIM.

Psalm 1:2-3

But his delight is in the law of the Lord, And in His law he meditates day and night. He will be like a tree firmly planted by streams of water, Which yields its fruit in its season And its leaf does not wither; And in whatever he does, he prospers.

Psalm 92:12-13

The righteous man will flourish like the palm tree, He will grow like a cedar in Lebanon. Planted in the house of the Lord, They will flourish in the courts of our God.

Ephesians 3:17-19

so that Christ may dwell in your hearts through faith; and that you, being rooted and grounded in love, may be able to comprehend with all the saints what is the breadth and length and height and depth, and to know the love of Christ which surpasses knowledge, that you may be filled up to all the fullness of God.

SIGNIFICANCE:

So, receive the WORDS of the ONE Good Shepherd who can both lovingly convict (goad) and establish us in Him each and every day.

17

Live Your Life With Purpose

Ecclesiastes 12:1

Remember also your Creator in the days of your youth, before the evil days come and the years draw near when you will say, "I have no delight in them"

Ecclesiastes 12:6-8

Remember Him before the silver cord is broken and the golden bowl is crushed, the pitcher by the well is shattered and the wheel at the cistern is crushed; then the dust will return to the earth as it was, and the spirit will return to

God who gave it. "Vanity of vanities," says the Preacher, "all is vanity!"

James 4:13-14

Come now, you who say, "Today or tomorrow we will go to such and such a city, and spend a year there and engage in business and make a profit." Yet you do not know what your life will be like tomorrow. You are just a vapor that appears for a little while and then vanishes away.

Yesterday was a tough day for us as a family. We lost my wife's older brother Daniel; he was 68 years young. He had been fighting the scourge of cancer for the past two years. He was a good man as far as worldly standards go. He was always there to lend a hand to neighbors and people in need. However, in the end, I am not sure he ever really found the purpose God had intended for his life. I know from talking with him over the 40+ years I knew him that when he was a sophomore in high school, he gave his life to Jesus at the height of the then-popular "Jesus Movement." Yet, as the Searcher said, many evil and trying days seemed to carry his heart away from the Creator. Like all of us, at times, he became distracted by the cares of life and just living day-to-day.

As the family gathered around his bed in what would be one last time to say our goodbyes, I could tell his body was shutting down as he went in and out of lucidity. I looked for an opportunity to speak to him one last time about where his heart stood with Jesus. In an awkward moment, when everyone was quiet, I spoke up. I said, "Dan, the Father is waiting for you today with open arms. Will you come back to Him now? Will you ask Jesus back into your heart and to forgive your sins?" You could have heard a pin drop in the room. At once, he came out of his fog and was of a clear mind. He was looking right into my eyes when someone else then interjected a sarcastic comment. He immediately told them to "shut up!" He then looked back at me, closed his eyes, and asked me to pray for him. I prayed at that moment that this prodigal son would come home and find rest and peace with the Father. Dan did not really say anything, yet gripped my hands very hard as I prayed. The sweet presence of Jesus filled that room at 2:20 p.m., and a few tears were shed.

Soon afterward, we all left as Dan drifted back into unconsciousness. At 10:00 p.m., he passed on into Eternity. I am not 100% sure of his return to the Father. In our conversations in his last couple of weeks, I could see he was full of a lot of shame and regrets that seemed to keep him at a distance from reconciliation with God. As I sit here and soberly ponder all of this, here are a few thoughts that I want to leave with you.

1. Never allow the cares and worries of life to carry you away from a vital relationship with the Father. Keep in close contact with Him daily. And if a day or two goes by and you find you have not talked with Him, just return to Him immediately. He understands. He will not punish you. He loves you!

Psalm 17:15

As for me, I shall behold Your face in righteousness; I will be satisfied with Your likeness when I awake.

1 John 4:16

We have come to know and have believed the love which God has for us. God is love, and the one who abides in love abides in God, and God abides in him.

2. Don't live a life of regret! Seek the Father for His purposes for you. It really is true: He has a plan for your life! Find His plan today and begin to act on it!

Jeremiah 29:11

"For I know the plans that I have for you," declares the LORD, "plans for welfare and not for calamity to give you a future and a hope."

3. Life is so short! It is way too short to allow grudges and hard feelings to keep you from loving your family and friends. Keep short accounts with people and God. Put down your pride, admit when you are wrong, and ask forgiveness. Even if you are NOT wrong, ask forgiveness.

Matthew 6:14-15

For if you forgive others for their transgressions, your heavenly Father will also forgive you. But if you do not forgive others, then your Father will not forgive your transgressions.

Ephesians 4:1-2

Therefore I, the prisoner of the Lord, implore you to walk in a manner worthy of the calling with which you have been called, with all humility and gentleness, with patience, showing tolerance for one another in love,

4. Take care of your body; it is the Temple of God. Get some exercise daily, eat nutritiously, and get at least 7 hours of sleep per night.

1 Corinthians 6:19

Do you not know that your body is a temple of the Holy Spirit who is in you, whom you have from God, and that you are not your own?

5. Express your love and appreciation for friends

and family often, as you never know when it may be the last time you see them.

1 Peter 5:14

Greet one another with a kiss of love. Peace be to you all who are in Christ.

SIGNIFICANCE:

I believe that Solomon sums up his "Search For Significance" well in the last two verses of the book Ecclesiastes:

Ecclesiastes 12:13-14 (NASB)

The conclusion, when all has been heard, is: fear God and keep His commandments, because this applies to every person. For God will bring every act to judgment, everything which is hidden, whether it is good or evil.

The End of the Matter

As I was on the internet this morning searching through various miscellaneous topics, on a whim, I typed in a search for "The most popular verse in The Book of Ecclesiastes." The first thing that showed up in my menu bar was a site called, "TopVerses.com," and in the very middle of their page in a big, black, bold font was:

Ecclesiastes 3:1 (NIV)

There is a time for everything, and a season for every activity under the heavens:

This site said this verse was the 380th most searched for passage in the Bible out of 31,105 searches on the internet. That is so very amazing to me! So, this verse about being aware of "time and seasons" and the importance they play in our lives is searched for in the top 1.22% of Bible verses people search for on the net! In this devotional journey we have been on, I am hoping this has been a "time and season" of discovery for you! I am believing and trusting you picked up this book for a purpose, and the Father has used it to stir some deep searchings within your own heart about the meaning and significance of your OWN life.

As I have read through this little devotional book many times now, preparing to make it presentable to you, some thoughts struck me, and I wish to leave them with you now:

1. It is very much okay to be completely honest with the Father about what you feel: the hurts, the anger, the pains, the disillusionments that you may be suffering in your life presently, or whenever they may assail you. If there was one lesson we can learn from Solomon, it is to "let our hair down," to say and express how we feel. So many of us have been in churches where people put on a good facade...You know how it goes, you ask them, "How are you this morning?"... They look back at you, smiling and say, "Great!" when all along they are miserable inside. We will never make progress in life or spiritually unless we can be honest and vulnerable with ourselves, The Father, and, hopefully, others. Real growth begins many times in recognizing our pain. We could call these circumstances and disappointments, "Growing Pains."

2. Sometimes "Ya just gotta sink to the bottom of the barrel" before you can begin to make any progress positively in your life. I believe that was the way Solomon lived. To me, it seemed throughout Ecclesiastes that he was on a mad dash to spend the most, buy the most, experience the most pleasure, trying anything and everything he could, in reckless abandonment. I believe he was indeed "Sold Out" to living in the utmost carnality possible! That may be you today, as you have read this book, maybe even in a skeptical way. It is my prayer that this humble treatise on Solomon and Ecclesiastes STOPS you cold in your tracks! I am praying that through all the reckless and irresponsible examples Solomon shared with us that you will search

your heart and know there is more to living life than "the lust of the flesh, the lust of the eyes, and the pride of life," as the Apostle John warned us about (1 John 2:16 KJV). This IS your time and season to come to the Father and know fulfillment, pleasures, peace, and contentment beyond anything you could ever experience in this life.

3. Finally, and most importantly of all, put into practice the good things you have learned in this journey. Make your peace with God, then go out in the world and BE SIGNIFICANT.

- "Be on Time." Have the wisdom to know the importance of the season you are living in, and allow the Father to guide you.

- Realize God has placed a longing and desire FOR HIM in your heart. Follow that and seek it out--it is how you were created.

- Be the comfort and solution others need, which means being aware of those who cross your path daily and what they may be going through.

- God says you are His own special PERFUME. He desires for your life to be not only a sweet savor to Him but to the world also.

- Be willing to SEE and experience the gift in adversity that He has for you when you experience it in life.

- Experience the blessing of being a generous giver.

Finally….

Ecclesiastes 12:13-14 (AMPC)

All has been heard; the end of the matter is: Fear God [revere and worship Him, knowing that He is] and keep His commandments, for this is the whole of man [the full, original purpose of his creation, the object of God's providence, the root of character, the foundation of all happiness, the adjustment to all inharmonious circumstances and conditions under the sun] and the whole [duty] for every man. For God shall bring every work into judgment, with every secret thing, whether it is good or evil.

Made in United States
North Haven, CT
01 July 2022

20835756R10063